COASTAL
── AUSTRALIA ──

COASTAL
AUSTRALIA

NICK RAINS

CONTENTS

FOREWORD

What is it that draws us to the coast? It certainly has a powerful allure, and one that has exercised a significant influence on modern Aussie culture. The vast majority of us live within an hour's drive of it. We flock to it in summer. On fair-weather weekends, we hook up the trailer and head to the nearest body of water to mess about in boats. We pay hundreds of thousands over the odds to live with a view of it. If we imagine paradise, pure white sand lapped by azure waters will more than likely be part of the vision. We really do like to be beside the seaside.

Australia is blessed with coastline – more than 35,000 kilometres of it. And that's excluding the islands, which account for a further 23,859 kilometres. Close to our biggest towns and cities, there's barely a skerrick of seafront that hasn't fallen victim to our watery obsession, but look a little harder, or, better still, ask the locals, and you'll still find hidden pockets of serenity. Even Sydney's legendary harbour has numerous quiet little beaches flanked by natural backdrops of sandstone and bush, all within striking distance of more than four million residents. In fact, 94 per cent of our coastline remains in its natural state.

Beyond the stretches of urban development, the coast runs mostly wild, oscillating between rocky promontories and pretty sandy beaches and punctuated by small towns and fishing villages. Every now and then, this rhythm is disrupted by dramatic geological features hewn by the pounding of the ocean. Along the Great Ocean Road, for instance, the Twelve Apostles are continually eroded by the merciless Southern Ocean; likewise the magnificent arc of the Bunda Cliffs on the Great Australian Bight, where the vast continent comes to an abrupt end. By contrast, the fraying margins of the remote Kimberley Coast are pummelled by the huge tidal movements of the continental shelf, while the granite and dolerite rock formations of the Freycinet Peninsula stand resolute in face of the violent storms and high winds that can whip up along Tasmania's east coast at any time of the year.

A passion to photograph the infinite variety and ever-changing moods of the Australian landscape gets Nick Rains out of bed before sunrise on many days of the year. This collection of his best coastal images reveals his talent for judging the light and locating the perfect vantage point from which to communicate the magnificent scale of these seascapes. In particular, his urban scenes perfectly capture those wonderful sensations of freedom and joy that epitomise a day at the beach. There is barely a corner of the island continent that hasn't found itself the focus of Nick's artistic eye – the frozen landscapes and distinctive wildlife of our distant subantarctic territories included – and so this magnificent book provides a truly comprehensive portrait of Australia's coast.

Chrissie Goldrick
Editor-in-Chief, *Australian Geographic* magazine

INTRODUCTION

If you visit the Australian Bureau of Statistics website and check out the various population distribution maps there, you will see quite clearly that most Australians live either along the south-east coast or on a small section of the west coast. Population densities around Sydney and Melbourne are around 6000–8000 people per square kilometre, whereas in the Red Centre the figure can be as low as 1 person per square kilometre. And, to throw some more startling statistics at you, around 85 per cent of all Australians live within 50km of the coast, while in Western Australia it's over 90 per cent, and in Tasmania a hard-to-believe 99 per cent!

Historically, civilisations have commonly developed along coastlines for all sorts of geographic and economic reasons: for example, trade routes, transport and food sources can all be easily developed around natural harbours and river mouths. Nevertheless, less than half the world's population lives within 100km of the coast, so Australia is somewhat unusual in this respect.

To understand why, take a look at the geography. The bulk of the Australian continent is dry, arid and difficult to exploit, whereas the south-eastern coastal areas, in particular, offer fresh water, alluvial plains and numerous safe harbours. So it's no surprise that we all live so close to the sea – that's where much of the good land is.

However, I think another factor is at work here too. You can call me a romantic, but I believe Australians also just like being near the ocean. Judging by the prices paid for houses with even a glimpse of the sea, it's clear that we are prepared to pay dearly for the privilege. Maybe it's a way of connecting with our evolutionary past, or maybe we just like the colour blue. I don't know the answer for sure, but the so-called urge for a sea change is clearly strong among retirees and anyone tired of the urban rat race.

Because Australia is such a large continent, its coastline shows a great deal of variation, ranging through mangrove swamps in the tropics, endless expanses of sand, rocky headlands, windswept sea cliffs, tranquil bays with white sandy beaches, and any combination thereof. In this book I have not tried to be comprehensive in my coverage, choosing instead to divide the content into 'styles' of shoreline. A geographer might wince at this, but as a photographer I am a visual organiser and, to me at least, Australia's shores fall neatly into the following five groups, though there is some overlap:

Urban: Coast near to where most of us live.

Tranquil: The sorts of places we would rather be when driving to work in the morning.

Wild: The type of wild and woolly coastline of which Australia has no shortage.

Remote: Amazing coastline that is far from anywhere.

Islands: Offshore landmasses – Australia has more than 8000 of them.

The locations I have chosen are both representative of their 'style', as well as visually appealing. Ranging from the cauldron of the seas around subantarctic Macquarie Island to the tidal flats of the Kimberley, and from the blue paradise of Eagle Bay in northern New South Wales to the rugged sea cliffs of Tasmania, this collection is a celebration of the diversity of Australia's amazing coastline.

Nick Rains

Viewed from Coolangatta Beach at dusk, tall buildings line the Gold Coast shoreline, in southern Queensland.

URBAN

FOR such a big country, Australia is still a heavily urbanised one, with roughly 90 per cent of the population living in towns and cities. A quick glance at a census map will also show that most live within a few dozen kilometres of the coast.

Luckily for their inhabitants, many of Australia's most densely populated coastal areas encompass beautiful stretches of coastline. Sydney is a prime example, with its spectacular harbour and iconic beaches, such as Bondi Beach – arguably one of the most famous in the entire world.

The photo of the surf carnival at Kurrawa Beach (p. 13), sums up our relationship with the coast – thousands of people congregating to compete in a surf lifesaving competition – and indicates just how many people actively swim and surf on beaches right beside our major cities. I took this photo from high up on the judges' podium. That bit of elevation meant that I could see further down the coast and get a sense of the scale of the operations. The rich blue sky and puffy white clouds further enhance the scene.

Saltwater swimming pools
flank Coogee Surf Life Saving
Club, Sydney.

an early-morning swim:
cold water, then hot coffee
– the Sydney beach lifestyle

On a hot, calm summer's day, surfers laze on boards off Clarks Beach, Byron Bay, New South Wales, waiting for a wave.

Seen from Lavender Bay, the bright lights of waterfront Luna Park add sparkle to this Sydney Harbour scene.

Rough conditions test competitors at a surf-lifesaving competition on the Gold Coast, Queensland.

*along the **ever-changing** shoreline,*
*there is **always** something*
***new** to see*

ABOVE Late afternoon's a great time to enjoy a stroll on Mooloolaba Beach, on the Sunshine Coast, Queensland.

RIGHT Storms brood offshore at dawn, near Caloundra on the Sunshine Coast, Queensland.

The Coastal Track in Noosa National Park, at Noosa, Queensland, takes in delightful, tranquil Tea Tree Bay.

Seen from the air, a surfer at Noosa, Queensland, makes the ride look effortless.

An afternoon game of beach football leaves its mark on Coolangatta Beach, on the Gold Coast, Queensland.

expanses of *golden sand* bring out
a *child's* sense of *fun* in everyone

Dicky Beach on the Sunshine Coast, Queensland, is named after the wreck of the SS *Dicky*, which ran aground here during a cyclone in 1893.

RIGHT It's another beautiful day in paradise at Airlie Beach, sailors' haven and gateway to the Whitsunday Islands, Queensland.

Cape Byron lighthouse, at Byron Bay, New South Wales, sits majestically on the easternmost point of the Australian mainland.

the *dawn* of *a* new day

never fails to move *us with*

the promise *of things to* come

Equipment and competitors line Kurrawa Beach during a surf-lifesaving competition on the Gold Coast, Queensland.

Clear Indian Ocean water makes beautiful Cottesloe Beach, in the western suburbs of Perth, a popular destination.

At Dolphin Point Lookout, on the Coastal Track in Noosa National Park, Queensland, the view opens out over Granite Bay.

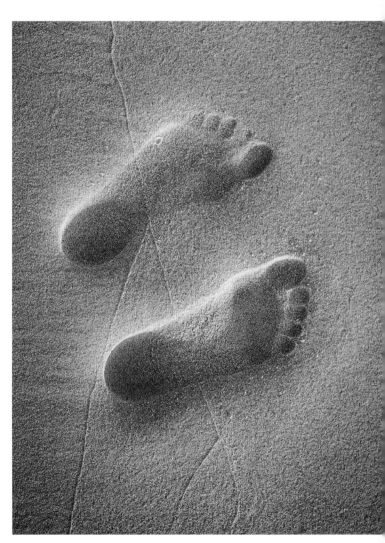

There is nothing like the feeling of sand between your toes and then the cool ocean washing over them.

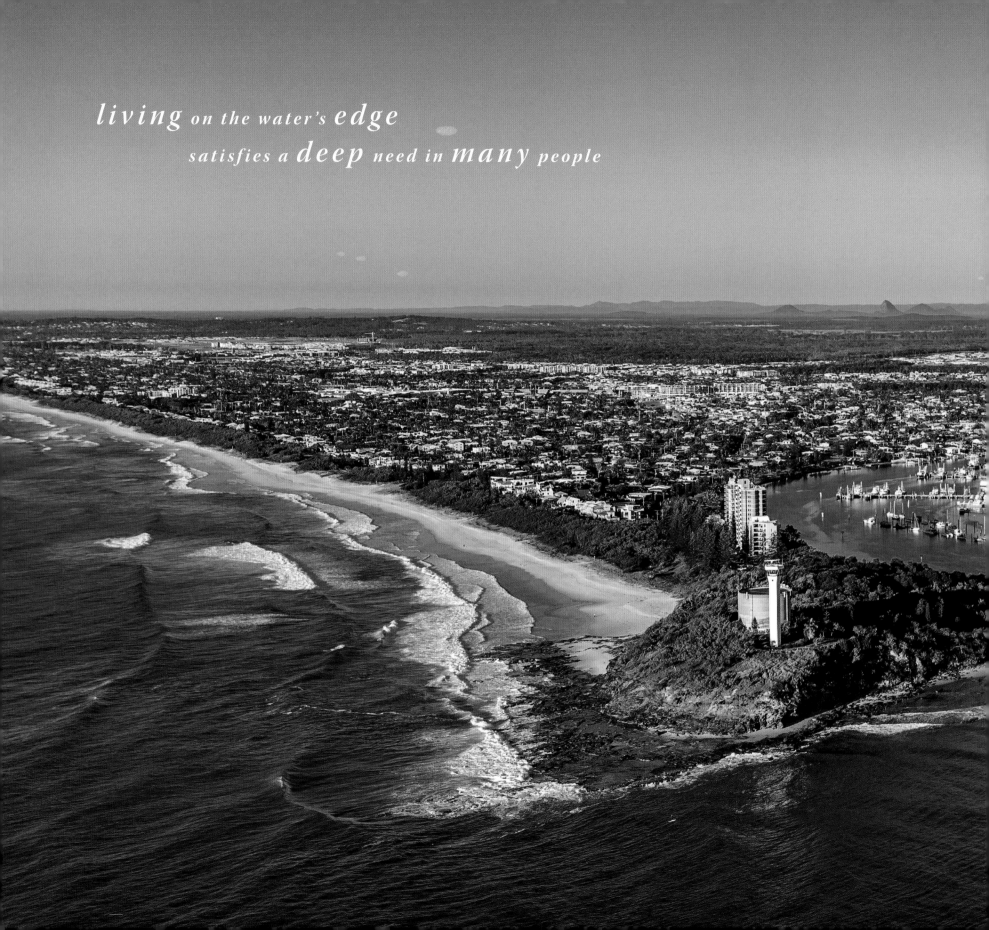

living on the water's *edge* satisfies *a* **deep** *need in* **many** people

Beacon Lighthouse crowns Point Cartwright, at the mouth of the Mooloolah River in Queensland. The Glasshouse Mountains are just visible in the distance.

ABOVE Dogs enjoy a late-afternoon romp in the water, at Mooloolaba Beach on the Sunshine Coast, Queensland.

RIGHT Little waves inspire giant leaps of joy at Queensland's Mooloolaba Beach.

FAR RIGHT Judging by the number of moorings and jetties, sailing is a popular pastime off the CBD and Battery Point in Hobart, Tasmania.

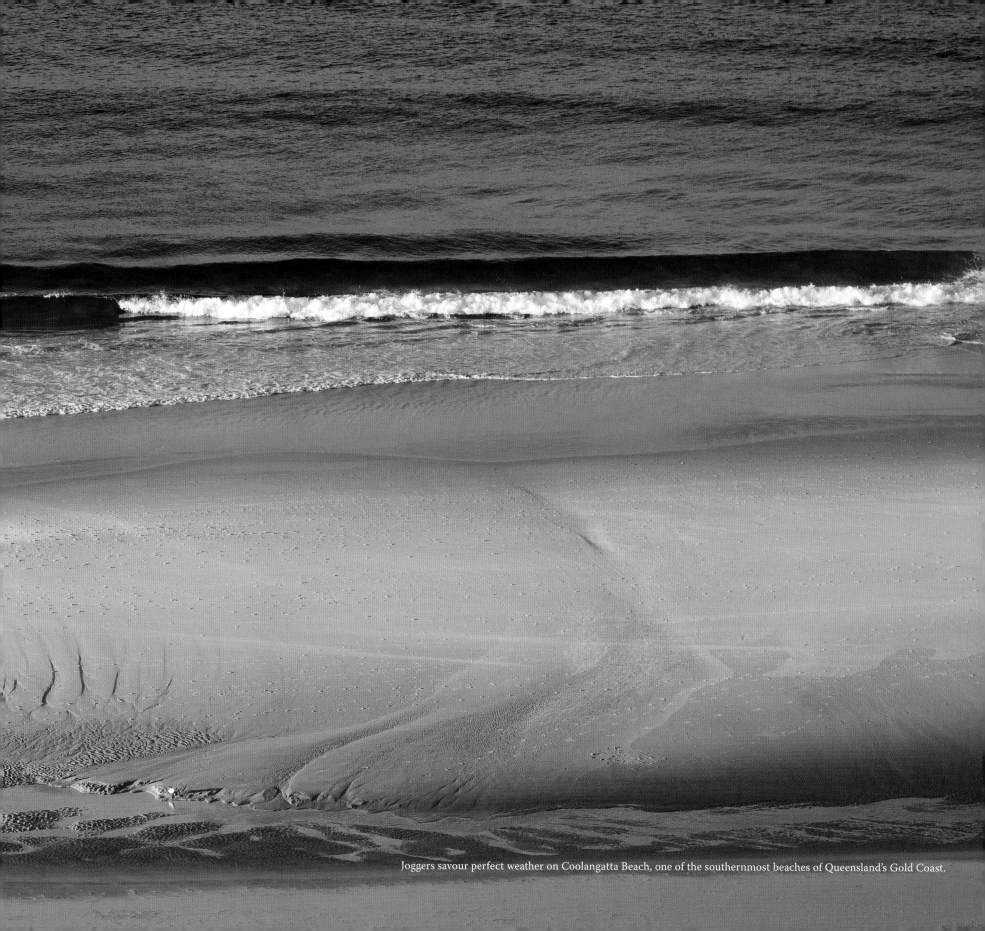

Joggers savour perfect weather on Coolangatta Beach, one of the southernmost beaches of Queensland's Gold Coast.

the break of *dawn*:
calm waters, *soothing* light,
and *solitude*

Historic Shorncliffe Pier, on the edge of Brisbane, stretches 350 metres out into Bramble Bay.

ABOVE Having put down roots, these grasses, near Noosa, Queensland, help stabilise the sand dunes.

OPPOSITE Pink dawn light tinges Macquarie Lighthouse, Australia's oldest lighthouse, near Watsons Bay, Sydney.

A long exposure captures the speed of clouds moving out
to sea from the Mornington Peninsula, Victoria.

Dawn light bathes Sydney Harbour and the city's central business district in a golden glow.

some cities are defined by their relationship with the coast

Adventurers ascend 'Beowulf' on a wild and windy day
at Whitewater Wall, Coles Bay, Tasmania.

WILD

THE Australian continent covers a colossal 7.7 million square kilometres and its coastline is more than 35,000 kilometres long. Our coast's diversity is mind-boggling. Some parts are relatively sheltered but others are pounded by the full force of the Pacific, Indian or Southern oceans, resulting in spectacularly sculpted landforms and dramatic vistas.

The east coast of Tasmania is one of the wildest stretches, with waves from the chilly Tasman Sea, powered by the Roaring Forties, hammering constantly on its shore. The cliffs around the Freycinet Peninsula are exposed to strong winds through much of the winter, but on calmer days, in the warmer seasons, it's possible to get out and get in some serious rock climbing, as on pages 36–7 and 66. This climb is called 'Beowulf' and it traverses the rock face above a sea-cave mouth, making it an intimidating ascent. Even photographing it was no trivial task, but luckily I used to rock climb myself and was (more or less) at home hanging over the abyss with my camera safely strapped to my hands.

rough seas, **strong** winds and **thick** clouds – *nature is* *always* in charge

'God beams', more correctly known as crepuscular rays, shine through the evening clouds at William Bay National Park, near Denmark, Western Australia.

Spray rises from the early-morning surf at Emerald Beach, New South Wales.

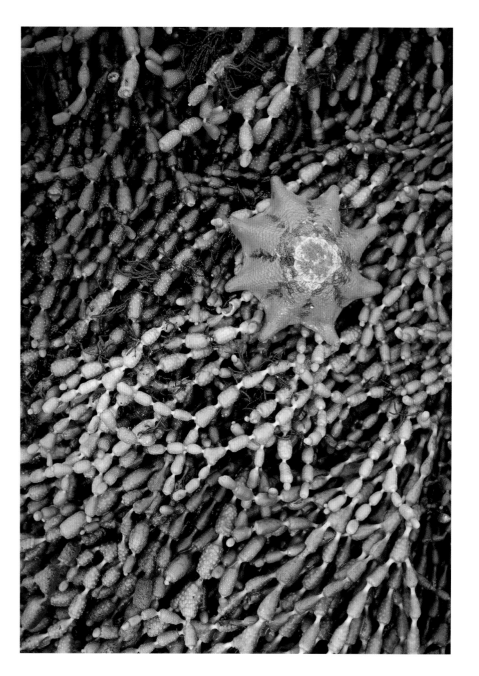

ABOVE This starfish washed up onto seaweed after a storm on Tasmania's east coast.

LEFT On a stormy morning, waves career and crash against Canal Rocks near Yallingup, Western Australia.

often startling in its clear hue,
the Southern Ocean has
a blue tint all its own

ABOVE High seas tossed this bluebottle, or Portuguese man o' war, onto Mandalay Beach in D'Entrecasteaux National Park, south of Manjimup, Western Australia.

RIGHT Seen from the air, waves and sands form sinuous patterns along Bremer Bay, Western Australia.

The granite outcrop known as Sugarloaf Rock juts out
of the sea near Dunsborough, Western Australia.

Gentle waves roll in steadily on a clear, calm day at Bremer Bay, Western Australia.

The rising sun silhouettes the spectacular eroded limestone stacks of the Twelve Apostles, in Port Campbell National Park, Victoria.

the *Victorian* coastline's *dazzling* beauty **belies** its more *treacherous* moods

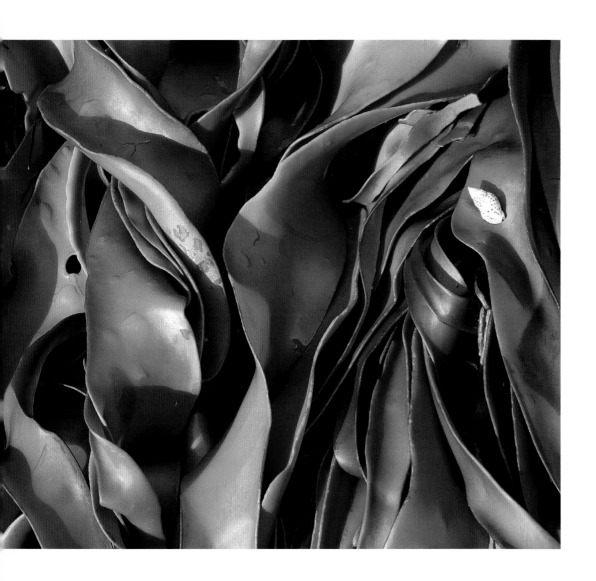

ABOVE Drying out in the sun, ocean sea kelp swathes a sandy beach on Tasmania's east coast.

RIGHT A pre-dawn storm cell looms ominously off the coast near Dunsborough, Western Australia.

Rocky ramparts resist the pounding waves, beneath a stormy sky at Emerald Beach, New South Wales.

coastal weather is ever *fickle*
– *just ask any* sailor

ABOVE Viewed from the jetty at Freycinet Lodge, Tasmania, a colossal roll cloud moves in over Coles Bay.

OPPOSITE All along the coast near Bicheno in Tasmania, red lichen splashes its intense colours across the rocks.

ABOVE The dramatic Zuytdorp Cliffs, near Denham in Western Australia, extend for 150 kilometres and are named after a Dutch ship wrecked here in 1712.

LEFT Cape Otway Lighthouse perches above a churning sea, on a stormy summer's day in western Victoria.

even when it **barely** *seems to* **move,** *the* **sea** *is at work,* **fashioning** *shapes from the* **shoreline**

Brooding clouds and a rising sun
transform the light at the Bay of Fires,
on the east coast of Tasmania.

ABOVE Jagged limestone cliffs drop abruptly into the Indian Ocean at Cape Keraudren Coastal Reserve, north of Port Hedland, Western Australia.

LEFT Water, sand, cloud and dawn light conspire to create a painterly scene in Walpole–Nornalup National Park, near Walpole, Western Australia.

Moonlight illuminates Twilight Beach near Esperance, Western Australia. Even the clouds can't dampen the intense blue of the ocean.

rippled sand or
clusters of living creatures:
nature loves patterns

ABOVE A circle of rock remains exposed at the centre of an enormous mass of molluscs, on Tasmania's east coast.

LEFT A storm approaches over the dunes at Fowlers Bay, South Australia. The bright rainbow at left is echoed by a fainter one at right.

Scaling coastal cliffs, high above a pounding swell, as here at Whitewater Wall, Coles Bay, Tasmania, demands expert technique and nerves of steel.

A full moon rises at sunset over the rough, rocky coastline at Wyadup, near Dunsborough, Western Australia.

A low sun picks out the shifting shapes of the sand dunes at
Fowlers Bay, South Australia, as a small storm front approaches.

Lusitania Bay, on Macquarie Island, is home to a vast rookery of King penguins.

wildness – distance from human settlements – is what some creatures really need to thrive

A lone rider makes the most of the swell at Yallingup, on the south-west coast of Western Australia.

Camels and passengers form a parade on Cable Beach. North-western Australia has the continent's best sunsets.

TRANQUIL

WARM, clear sea water, white sand and blue sky. It's an image that epitomises tranquillity and one that draws people from far and wide to Australia. We are blessed with some of the best beaches in the world and you don't really need to search hard to find one. Almost all Australian states claim they have the best places for kicking off your shoes, cooling off in the sea and enjoying the peace and quiet, and the truth is that in this respect they are all winners!

Beaches are not the only tranquil places on the coast, however. Any part of the shoreline, on a calm day with light winds, can be extremely peaceful – there's something about gently lapping water that calms the nerves.

Eagle Bay, in the south-west corner of Western Australia (p. 82), is relatively sheltered from the full force of the Indian Ocean; it's also quite shallow and has very clean white sand. With the water being so clear and the sunlight reflecting back off the sand, the intensity of the blue is so strong that it is extremely hard to photograph.

at dawn the full, bright moon
always seems to sit low
on the horizon

The moon rises over Twilight
Beach, near Esperance,
Western Australia, adding a
silvery sheen to sea and sky.

Low clouds hang over Coles Bay, on the east coast of Tasmania. With no wind, the water is as smooth as glass.

Eastern grey kangaroos speed towards the cover of bushes, near Emerald Beach, New South Wales.

RIGHT Giant lichen-covered boulders hem a
secluded pool in William Bay National Park,
near Denmark, Western Australia.

The Indian Ocean displays dazzling shades of blue, at Eagle Bay, north of Dunsborough, Western Australia.

small details and grand vistas
can be equally appealing

ABOVE Glossy, smooth stones cover a beach in Freycinet National Park, on the east coast of Tasmania.

RIGHT The jetty at Freycinet Lodge, in eastern Tasmania, reaches out into a still Coles Bay morning.

Mimosa Rocks National Park in New South
Wales is named after the paddlesteamer
Mimosa, which ran aground here in 1863.

ABOVE On a hot day at Castle Rock Beach, Dunsborough, Western Australia, some shade is essential.

LEFT Mirror-like water reflects the evening sky on the Huon River, south-west of Hobart, Tasmania.

not a **sound**, *except the* **lapping** *surf and the* **gentle** *creak of the* **rigging**

Passengers enjoy a spectacular sunset from the deck of a restored pearl lugger, off Cable Beach, Broome, Western Australia. How idyllic is that?

ABOVE A grey egret warily eyes the kayaking photographer at Moulting Lagoon, near Coles Bay, in eastern Tasmania.

RIGHT Early morning at Palm Cove, north of Cairns in Queensland, provides a perfect setting for quiet contemplation.

The appropriately named Blue Haven Beach, near Esperance, Western Australia, is reached via a walking track and a steep stairway.

ABOVE Eastern grey kangaroos graze on Look at Me Now headland, Emerald Beach, New South Wales.

LEFT Observatory Point and Lookout near Esperance, Western Australia, offers magnificent views and is a great place for whale-watching.

the *clear* evening *skies of the* **north** *seem*
to produce a **greater** *intensity of* **colour**

Night descends on a still, clear evening at Denham,
on the shore of Shark Bay, Western Australia.

Sunrise gilds the ocean off Mission Beach,
Queensland, with Dunk Island still in shadow.

The setting sun lights up sky and sea in
shades of red, orange and gold, as seen from
Shell Beach, in Shark Bay, Western Australia.

in the tropics, *the* sea *can be*
so calm *it seems almost* artificial

ABOVE Seagulls line up on a jetty railing at The Entrance, New South Wales.

RIGHT Crepuscular rays create a dazzling display of light at Trial Bay, New South Wales.

The estuary of the Red Rock River, north of Coffs Harbour,
New South Wales, is a beautiful spot for fishing and swimming.

A quiet inlet provides a sheltered mooring for fishing boats on the Bird River at Bridport in northern Tasmania.

REMOTE

The dark shadows of vast seagrass meadows lie just offshore,
in this aerial view of Shark Bay, Western Australia.

GIVEN that Australia has such a long coastline, it's not surprising that some of its most beautiful beaches are in the middle of nowhere. The Western Australian coast in particular has a huge range of perfect white-sand beaches so far from the cities that almost no-one visits them. Stay for days and you may not see a living soul the whole time.

Beaches don't get any more remote than Sandy Bay on Macquarie Island (p. 126). The island is two or three days by ship south of Hobart and, at only 34 kilometres by 5 kilometres, is little more than a speck in the ocean. What it lacks in size, however, it makes up for in drama, as the coast is extremely forbidding and the weather is usually vile.

I was lucky to be there on a fine day, when the temperature soared to about 7°C and the penguins were lying panting in the heat. The noise (and smell) was astonishing, but the impression I came away with was that of the overwhelming richness of life there – over 40,000 breeding pairs of seals, sea lions and elephant seals, plus hundreds of thousands of king and royal penguins and maybe 3.5 million breeding seabirds.

*a **coastal** fringe **fashioned** by **sea**, **wind** and **rain***

Angel Island near the Burrup Peninsula, in the Pilbara, Western Australia, is a sacred site for Indigenous Australians.

The multicoloured wagons of a goods train stand out starkly against the blue-grey
backdrop of the Dutchmans Stern range, north-east of Port Augusta, South Australia.

ABOVE A curious shark shadows our boat on the Berkeley River, near the Kimberley Coast, Western Australia.

LEFT The geological structure of the landscape is clearly visible in cliffs along Talbot Bay, on the Kimberley Coast, Western Australia.

At Montgomery Reef, on the
Kimberley Coast, Western Australia,
the rapidly changing tide forms
'horizontal waterfalls' over the
exposed reef.

ancient visitors left their mark;
today we try to leave no trace

ABOVE Ancient ochre Bradshaw (or Gwion Gwion) figures decorate sandstone cave walls along the Berkeley River, on the Kimberley Coast, Western Australia.

RIGHT This tidal coral cay on the outer Great Barrier Reef is accessible only by boat and only at low tide. At the right time, it's a great spot for a swim.

Dawn light bathes Hearsons
Cove, on the Burrup Peninsula,
near Dampier, Western Australia.

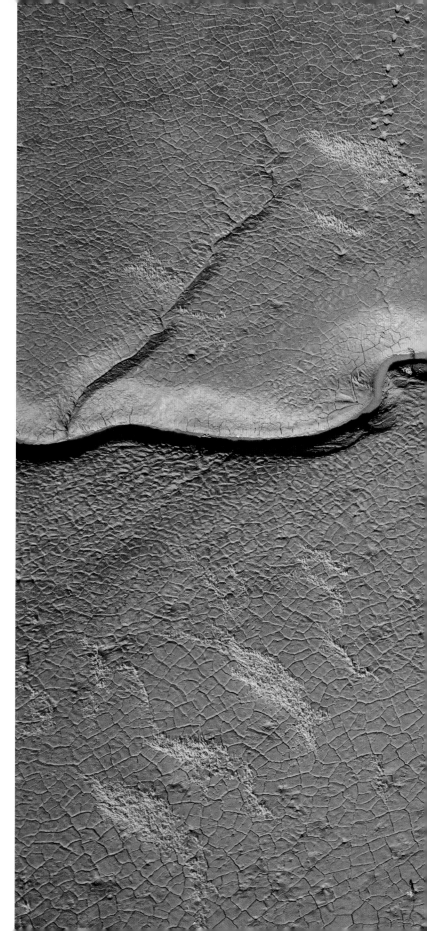

ABOVE The wreckage of a World War II US Air Force transport plane still lies at Vansittart Bay, on the Kimberley Coast, Western Australia.

RIGHT Viewed from the air, winding tidal creeks and dry mudflats form extraordinary abstract patterns in the East Kimberley, Western Australia.

Royal penguins and southern elephant seals enjoy a rare day of sunshine at Sandy Bay, on Macquarie Island, roughly midway between Australia and Antarctica.

three days by ship from *anywhere,* *Macquarie Island* is as *remote* as it gets

ABOVE Approximately 60 kilometres long, Shell Beach, in Shark Bay, Western Australia, is made up of billions of shells that have washed up over thousands of years.

RIGHT Mangroves and mudflats fringe the Hunter River where it winds through the Mitchell Plateau, near the Kimberley Coast, Western Australia.

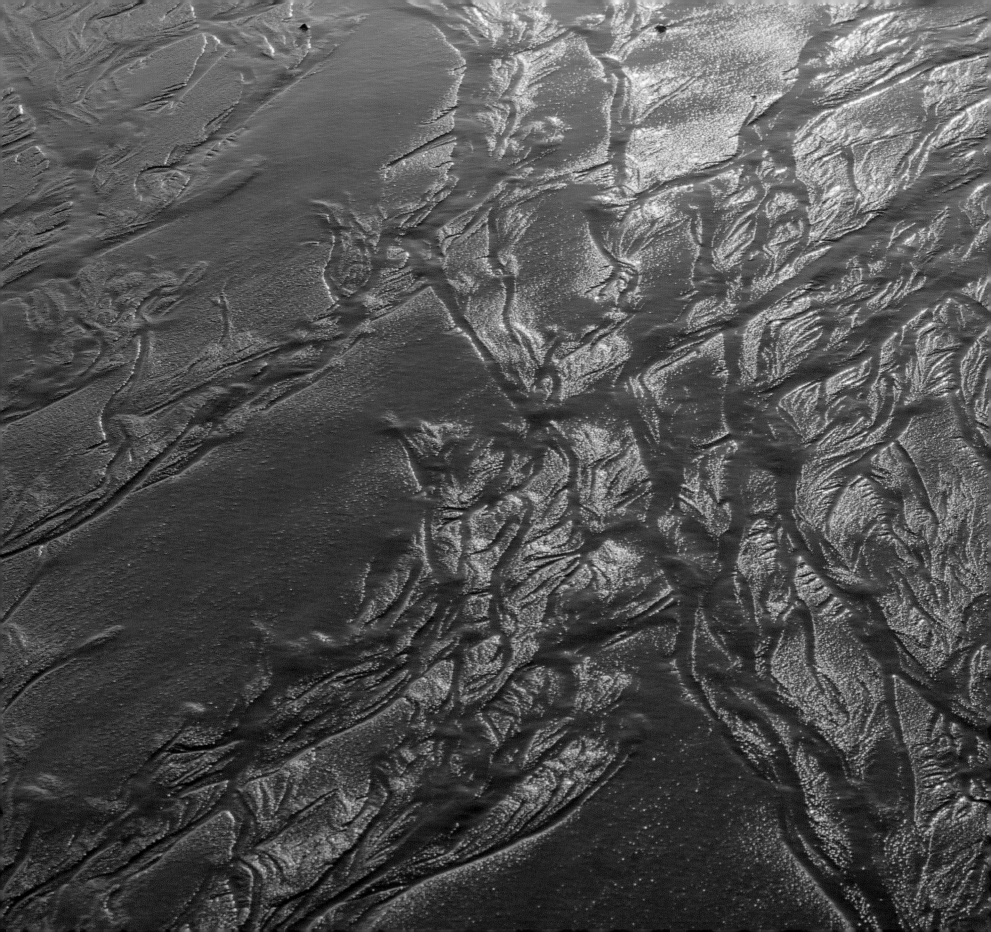

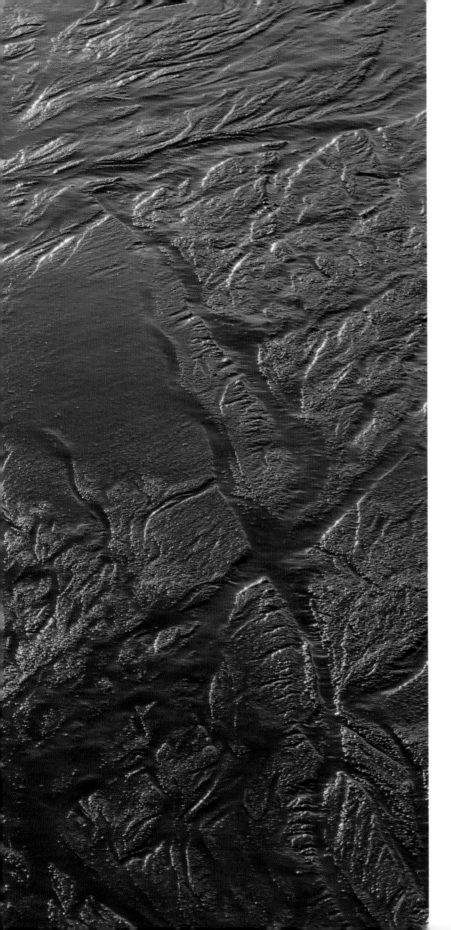

ABOVE A shell is left high and dry at Vansittart Bay, on the Kimberley Coast, Western Australia.

LEFT Sunrise highlights patterns in the sand, at Honeymoon Cove, Point Samson, Western Australia.

the **play** *of sunlight on the* **Kimberley's** *rockscapes and* **vast** *skies is* **endlessly** *fascinating*

The red rock of Raft Point, in the Kimberley region of Western Australia.

At the end of the wet season, drainage channels fan out across the drying mudflats of Cambridge Gulf, in the Kimberley, Western Australia.

scorched rocks are cooled
by cascading
wet-season waters

The Berkeley River, on Western Australia's Kimberley Coast, tumbles down red cliffs towards the Timor Sea.

Intensely red rocks border the white sands of Cape Leveque,
on the Dampier Peninsula in northern Western Australia.

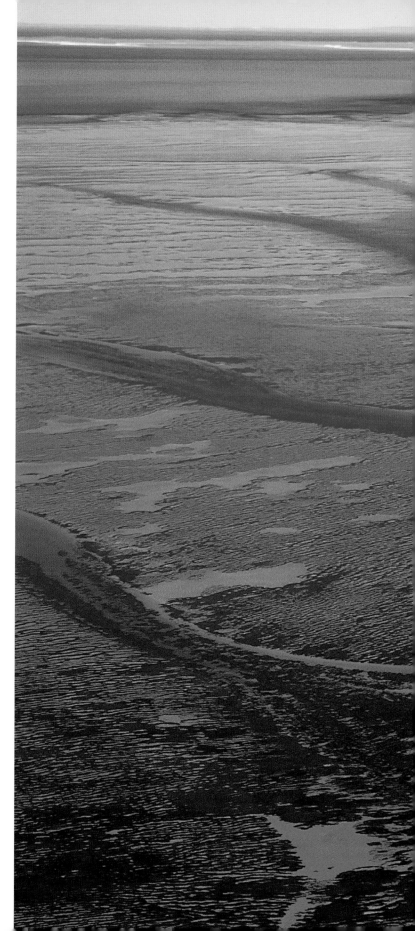

ABOVE Seen from the air, tidal rivulets meander through mudflats in the East Kimberley, Western Australia.

RIGHT Deep channels carve 'highways' through the dense seagrass meadows of Shark Bay, Western Australia.

Cruising past spectacular King George River Falls in the Kimberley, Western Australia, provides a wonderful sense of the region's grandeur.

red and blue are the colours that, in so many ways, define Australia

A dramatic cloudscape enhances the sunset at Eighty Mile Beach, on the north-west coast of Western Australia. This 220 kilometre stretch of sand is an important refuge for migratory shorebirds, as well as flatback turtles.

warm, sheltered water and a brisk
but steady breeze – a sailor's dream

A small sailing boat cuts across Catseye Bay, off the coast of Hamilton Island, in the Whitsunday Islands, Queensland, on a perfect sunny day.

ISLANDS

AUSTRALIA is officially a continent, not an island, but around its fringes lie 8222 actual islands, ranging from mere rocky outcrops to gargantuan Melville Island, which is twice the size of the ACT. While the images in the following pages show only a tiny fraction of the total, I hope they at least give a sense of the sheer variety and beauty of these places.

Lady Elliot Island (pp. 160, 174–5 and 180) is the archetypal desert island, a tiny coral cay surrounded by fringing reef, just big enough to act as a home to permanent vegetation and huge colonies of seabirds. It also manages to accommodate an airstrip, so you can fly there from Bundaberg, as I did on some of my visits.

Lady Elliot is world-renowned for its diving, but, for me, being able to walk around the island in under an hour is the main attraction. Once you are away from the small resort buildings, it's easy to imagine you are a million miles from anywhere, on a deserted beach with only the sand between your toes and an impossibly blue seascape all around.

Orange clownfish flit among the sea anemones,
on a section of the Great Barrier Reef near the
Whitsunday Islands, Queensland.

Rhapsody in Blue might be an apt title for this photograph of
Whitehaven Beach and Hill Inlet, on Whitsunday Island, Queensland.

in photographs some *places look too* good *to be* true
– until you visit *them in* person

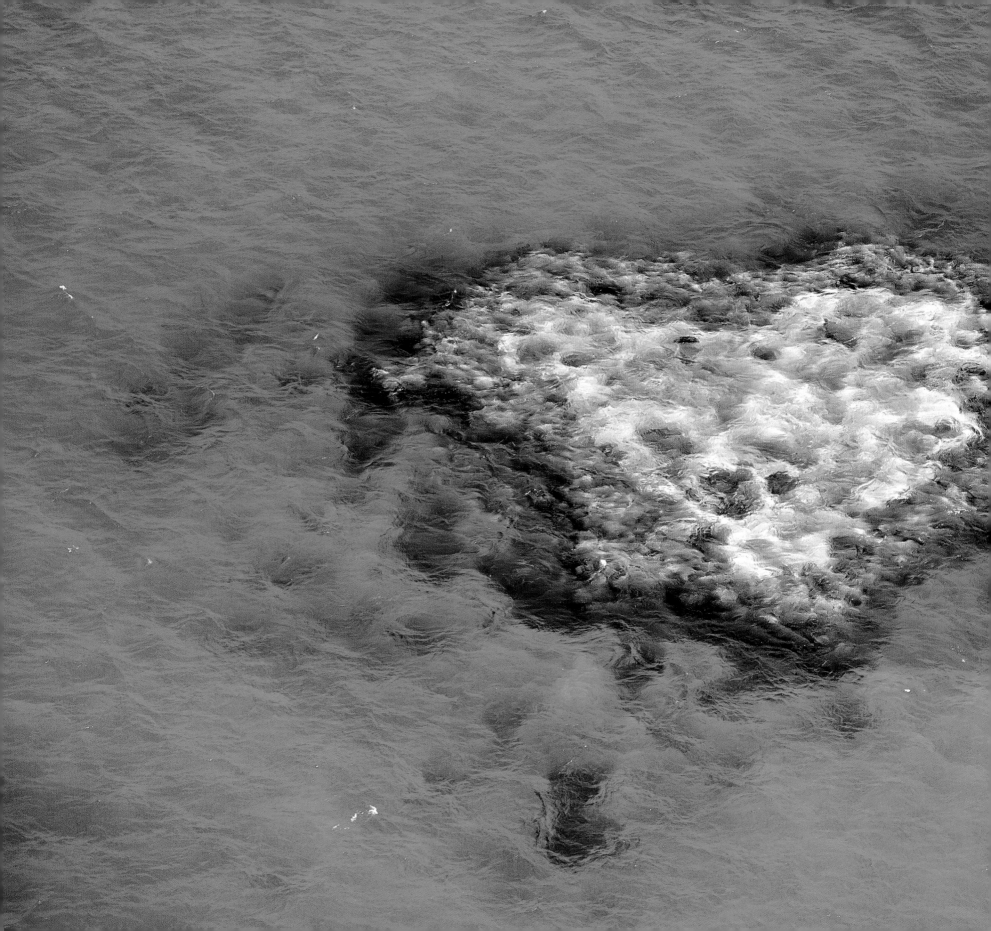

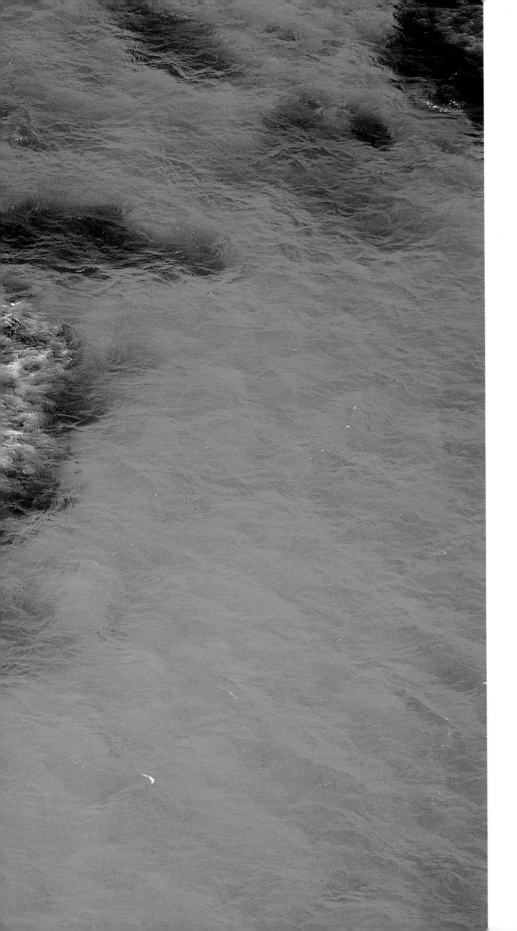

ABOVE Indigenous art, including first-contact art and Wandjina figures, adorns rock faces on Bigge Island, in the Bonaparte Archipelago, Western Australia.

LEFT Heart Reef, part of Hardy Reef, near the Whitsunday Islands, Queensland, is best appreciated from the air.

A dramatic view of a stormy dawn is revealed on the North Gorge Walk on North Stradbroke Island, Queensland.

slow down: *you're on* '*Island Time*'

ABOVE Who could resist building sandcastles on pristine Whitehaven Beach, on Queensland's Whitsunday Island?

RIGHT Tangalooma Resort on Moreton Island, Queensland, is only a short ferry ride away from Brisbane.

The sea's edge reflects a spectacular dawn sky on
Moreton Island, Queensland.

ABOVE Clear waters around Lady Elliot Island, on the Great Barrier Reef, make it easy to spot dramatic sealife, such as this blue starfish.

RIGHT A lone angler makes the best of the fading light in narrow Pumicestone Passage, between the mainland and Bribie Island, Queensland.

Blue sea and sky envelop the remote
Kingsmill Islands, off the Kimberley
Coast, Western Australia.

rich, ᴄᴏɴᴛʀᴀsᴛɪɴɢ *colours*
startle ᴛʜᴇ ᴠɪsɪᴛᴏʀ
ᴀᴛ *every* ᴛᴜʀɴ

All Saints Chapel perches on a hillside overlooking Catseye Bay,
on Hamilton Island, in Queensland's Whitsunday Islands.

LEFT Seen from on high, the coral structures of the Great Barrier Reef form lace-like patterns.

Sail around Queensland's Whitsunday Islands and you can visit
stunning secluded beaches, like this one on Hook Island.

A major landmark on the east coast of Fraser Island, Queensland, is the wreck of the SS *Maheno*, which came aground here in 1935.

ABOVE New Zealand fur seals often haul out on the shore of Carnac Island, off the coast near Perth.

RIGHT Hardy Reef, off the coast of northern Queensland, offers perfect conditions for snorkelling.

Countless freshwater creeks cut across the main
eastern beach on Fraser Island, Queensland.

beneath the tranquil surface,
another, submarine world teems with life

Crystal-clear water and pristine coral reefs lie just 10 metres
from the cabins on Lady Elliot Island, Queensland.

ABOVE Uninhabited and seldom visited, Winyalkan Island lies off one of the most remote parts of the Kimberley Coast, Western Australia.

LEFT The aptly named Remarkable Rocks, on Kangaroo Island, South Australia, are a collection of oddly shaped, wind-sculpted granite formations.

Passing sailors traditionally leave mementos at the rustic Percy Island Yacht Club – also known as the Percy Hilton – on Middle Percy Island, Queensland.

Lady Elliot Island, along with Lady Musgrave Island, marks the southern limit of the Great Barrier Reef.